UNDERSTANDING BIBLE TEACHING

God's Kingdom & Church

F F Bruce MA, DD

Scripture Union

47 Marylebone Lane, London W1 6AX

Wm. B. Eerdmans

225 Jefferson Avenue, Grand Rapids, Michigan

ISBN 0 85421 706 1 (Scripture Union)
ISBN 0 8028 1770 X (Wm. B. Eerdmans)

Printed in Great Britain at the Benham Press
by William Clowes & Sons Limited, Colchester and Beccles

General Introduction

There are many commentaries on the Biblical text and there are many systematic studies of Christian doctrine, but these studies are unique in that they comment on selected passages relating to the major teachings of the Bible. The comments are designed to bring out the doctrinal implications rather than to be a detailed verse by verse exposition, but writers have always attempted to work on the basis of sound exegetical principles. They have also aimed to write with a certain devotional warmth, and to demonstrate the contemporary relevance of the teaching.

These studies were originally designed as a daily Bible reading aid and formed part of Scripture Union's Bible Characters and Doctrines series. They can, of course, still be used in this way but experience has shown that they have a much wider use. They have a continued usefulness as a summary and exposition of Biblical teaching arranged thematically, and will serve as a guide to the major passages relating to a particular doctrine.

Writers have normally based their notes on the RSV text but readers will probably find that most modern versions are equally suitable. Many, too, have found them to be an excellent basis for group Bible study. Here the questions and themes for further study and discussion will prove particularly useful—although many individuals will also find them stimulating and refreshing.

ONE

The Kingdom of God in the Old Testament

1: 'A Kingdom of Priests and a Holy Nation'

Exodus 19

The Israelites had seen the sovereign power of God in action in the victory which He won for them at the Red Sea. The song in which they celebrated this victory ended with the affirmation: 'The LORD will reign for ever and ever' (Exod. 15.18). This is the first explicit mention of the Kingdom of God in the Bible, and from it we learn that His Kingdom is not to be understood territorially (as when we speak of the kingdom of England) but in the sense of His royal dominion, exercised over nature and men alike—over nature, as was seen in His curbing the Red Sea, and over men, both in His vindication of those who put their trust in Him and in His judgement on their enemies. Now, in the third month after that revelation of His kingship, the people reach Mount Sinai and learn more of what this implies in practice for those who acknowledge Him as their King. They had already witnessed the overthrow of the Egyptians and begun to experience their God's protecting guidance: 'I bore you on eagles' wings,' He says, 'and brought you to myself' (4)—a notable figure of speech, repeated in the Song of Moses (Deut. 32.11 f.). Now they were to learn that He had done this for them in order that they might be His own people, bound to Him in covenant loyalty, 'a kingdom of priests and a holy nation' (6). These words find an echo throughout the Bible; we shall come upon later echoes of them in 1 Pet. 2.9 and Rev. 5.10. We need not press too sharp a distinction between a 'kingdom of priests' and a 'holy nation', but we can sum up the meaning of the whole phrase by saying that the people of God are to represent Him on earth and to enter His presence as worshippers. This was God's plan for Israel: other nations would form a proper estimate of His holiness as they saw it reflected in the life of Israel, and it was Israel's privilege, as the chosen race, to draw near to God as representatives of mankind. The only hope for the realization of this ideal was Israel's acceptance of God's conditions: 'obey my voice and keep my covenant' (5). Israel

5

undertook to accept these conditions, and so, amid circumstances which emphasized the holiness of the God with whom they had to do, God gave them His law, the constitution of their covenanted existence. When the law had been given, Israel pledged obedience to it, and the covenant community was solemnly inaugurated (24.3–8).

Question: What do we learn of the nature of God and His covenant from the fact that He did not abrogate it when His people proved unable to keep it?

2: The Chosen People

Deuteronomy 7

The generation of Israelites that witnessed the deliverance from Egypt and the giving of the law at Sinai had passed away. A new generation had grown up, and only the oldest among them could remember the great events that had taken place in their childhood, forty years before. Hence it was necessary that this new generation should be confronted with the covenant claims of God, the more so as their predecessors had so dismally proved their inability to fulfil their undertaking to obey God and observe His laws. Now they were on the eve of entry into the promised land, where the temptations to forget the covenant would be even greater than those to which their predecessors had succumbed in the wilderness. Moses therefore summoned them before him in the plains of Moab to recapitulate the law which the previous generation had received from God, and to impress them with the solemnity of being God's covenant people (Deut. 5–11). He reminds them (6) that they are His *holy* people; He tells them for the first time that they are His *chosen* people.

Why did God choose Israel 'to be a people for his own possession, out of all the peoples that are on the face of the earth' (6)? It was not for any reason that might have flattered their self-esteem; indeed, had He looked for such a reason, He would have found none. It was because He loved them on His own initiative, because He was mindful of the oath He had sworn to their forefathers—Abraham, Isaac and Jacob—that He chose them (7 f.). He chose them, in other words, by His sheer grace.

But to be God's chosen people does not constitute a passport to a life of ease; it imposes formidable responsibilities (9–11). Those whom He chooses are called to 'love him and keep his commandments to a thousand generations', to exhibit something of His personal holiness in their own lives. As the subject is developed throughout the Bible, we learn that those who are chosen by God's grace are chosen not only to be holy but also to serve Him in a variety of ways and to be the vehicle of His blessing to others.

Meditation:

> *Chosen, not for good in me,*
> *Wakened up from wrath to flee,*
> *Hidden in the Saviour's side,*
> *By the Spirit sanctified,*
> *Teach me, Lord, on earth to show*
> *By my love, how much I owe.*

(R. M. M'Cheyne)

3: 'Thine is the kingdom'

1 Chronicles 29.10–25

For Israel the process of taking possession of the promised land was long and arduous, stretching over several generations, punctuated by many setbacks. Not until the reign of David was the process completed; under him God gave His people rest from all their enemies round about (2 Sam. 7.1). Sitting at peace in his palace, David conceived the plan of building a temple worthy of God in Jerusalem, which he had captured and selected as his capital city. He was told, however, that the privilege of building such a temple would not be his; it would be reserved for his son and successor. The closing chapters of 1 Chronicles (22–29) depict David, at the end of his reign, gathering the materials for the temple, so that Solomon his son might start to build it with the minimum of delay when he mounted the throne. The provision of such costly materials involved lavish expenditure, not only from the royal treasury but on the part of the people, who contributed generously to the work.

When all the preparation that David could make was finished, a service of dedication was held. King and people had 'offered willingly' and abundantly, and they enjoyed the gladness which accompanies such spontaneous liberality. The king led the act of worship in which the gifts were dedicated to God, acknowledging that the donors were only giving back to God what He had first given to them: 'All things come from thee, and of thy own have we given thee' (14). But in the dedication of their gifts

David and his subjects were dedicating themselves, in effect, if not in so many words, renewing their ancestral covenant with God. They knew themselves to be short-lived sojourners on earth: 'our days . . . are like a shadow, and there is no abiding' (15). But the God to whom they dedicated themselves was the supreme, eternal and universal King and (although this does not find actual expression here) it is by knowing themselves to be caught up into His immortal life that His people find the frustrations of their earth-bound span of life overcome and transcended.

Meditation: When the poverty-stricken Macedonian Christians 'gave according to their means . . . and beyond their means, of their own free will', Paul explained their action thus: 'first they gave themselves to the Lord, and to us by the will of God' (2 Cor. 8.3, 5).

4: 'The Lord of all the earth'

Psalm 97

'The Lord reigns' is a recurring confession in this part of the Psalter, which probably derived it from the temple worship. God had reigned as King from eternity: 'thy throne is established from of old; thou art from everlasting' (Psa. 93.2). But there were occasions in the annually repeated liturgy of Israel when His kingship was specially celebrated, and the acclamation 'The Lord reigns' (or, as it may be rendered, 'The Lord has become king') could belong primarily to such occasions.

While God manifested His kingship uniquely in the life of His people Israel, that did not mean (as Israel's neighbours imagined) that the gods of the surrounding nations exercised a comparable sovereignty over the communities that worshipped them. The God of Israel was the King of *all* nations: He who brought Israel up from Egypt to possess the land of Canaan also brought the Syrians and the Philistines from their former abodes to the lands which they currently occupied (Amos 9.7). So in this psalm, before God's relation to His own people is introduced, His sovereignty over the world is emphasized. This sovereignty is not based on naked power: 'righteousness and justice are the foundation of his throne' (2) in relation to the world as much as in relation to Israel. He whose law was imparted to Israel amid the 'clouds and thick darkness' of Sinai, with fire and lightning flashing forth (2–4), reveals Himself in

8

the same character to the universe. The worship of false gods is therefore as impermissible for other nations as it is for Israel. His own people rejoice when His judgements are abroad in the earth (cf. Isa. **26**.9). But let them reflect that His favour does not rest on them regardless of their conduct: 'the LORD loves those who hate evil' (10).

*Question: Is it still true that 'clouds and thick darkness are round about him' (2), or has the coming of Christ made a difference for us? Consider the significance here of the rending of the veil in Mark **15**.38, and the unconcealed glory in 2 Cor. **3**.18; **4**.6.*

5: 'The Lord has chosen Zion'

Psalm 132

From the wilderness period onwards the Ark of the Covenant was the palladium of the God of Israel in the midst of His people's life. It was the token of His presence, the throne of His invisible royalty. After it had accompanied the Israelites through the wilderness it was enshrined as the centre of their inter-tribal life at various sanctuaries in Canaan, latterly at Shiloh. But a time came when the Ark was treated as a magic talisman, and the people had to learn that its mere presence among them did not guarantee the help of God, and that God's presence in its turn was independent of the Ark. They had to learn this the hard way, first when the Ark was captured in battle by the Philistines and then, on its return, relegated to a place of obscurity during Samuel's career as judge. But with the accession of David, and his choice of Jerusalem as his capital, a new conception of king-ship was introduced in Israel. The God of Israel remained the nation's King, but His sovereignty was now manifested and mediated through His anointed servant who held royal power by His grace. David resolved to emphasize this aspect of his royalty by making Jerusalem not only his own capital but the capital of Israel's God, 'the city of the great King' (Psa. **48**.2). Therefore he brought the Ark out of its long seclusion at Kiriath-jearim and installed it with joyful ceremony in the tent-shrine which he had erected for it on Mount Zion, hard by his own palace (2 Sam. **6**.1–19). David's oath to provide in Jerusalem 'a dwelling place for the Mighty One of Jacob' (5), which is not recorded in the historical narrative, was thus fulfilled.

Verses 6, 7 speak of the preparations for moving the Ark:

'Ephrathah' refers to David's native Bethlehem (cf. Mic. **5.2**), and in 'the fields of Jaar' we have a poetical designation of Kiriath-jearim. According to 2 Chron. **6.41**, 42, the invocation of vs. 8–10 was recited at the dedication of Solomon's temple.

But the psalm itself dates from a time when the glories of David's reign were becoming a fading memory. The psalmist endeavours to revive his own faith and that of his fellows by recalling not so much David's oath to God as God's oath to David, communicated through the prophet Nathan, that his descendants would enjoy the kingship in perpetuity if they kept the covenant, and His oath to Zion, that it would be His dwelling place for ever. How God's oath to David was fulfilled in the resurrection and enthronement of Christ we may read in Acts **2.30**-32. How His oath to Zion is fulfilled we may read in Eph. **2.19**-22 and similar New Testament passages which speak of the spiritual sanctuary of living men and women which God has chosen for His dwelling place.

Meditation:
> *Zion enjoys her Monarch's love,*
> *Secure against the threatening hour;*
> *Nor can her firm foundation move,*
> *Built on His faithfulness and power.*

(I. Watts)

6: 'An everlasting kingdom'
Psalm 145

This is an acrostic poem: its successive verses begin with the 22 letters of the Hebrew alphabet in their proper sequence. The verse beginning with the Hebrew letter *Nun* has been accidentally lost in the traditional Hebrew text; fortunately it has been preserved by other ancient witnesses and appears in RSV as the last two lines of v. 13. In the Hebrew Psalter found in 1956 in Cave 11 at Qumran each verse of this psalm is followed by the refrain: 'Blessed is the Lord, and blessed is his name for ever and ever'—not part of the original text but added as a congregational response when the psalm was used in public worship.

It is appropriate that an acrostic psalm should run the whole gamut of the majesty and glory of God's Kingdom, from A to Z, so to speak. The changes are rung on the splendour of God's greatness and power and the wonder of His creative works, on the one hand, and on His kindness to 'all that he has made' (9) on the other. It is He who provides food for all His creatures

(15 f.), but to His own people 'who call upon him in truth' He has revealed Himself as One who is near them, hears their petitions and sends them salvation (18 f.). This bringing together of God's infinite power in creation and His tender care for individual human beings is paralleled in other psalms; cf. Psa. 147.3, 4: 'He heals the brokenhearted, and binds up their wounds; he determines the number of the stars, he gives to all of them their names.'

With the final establishment of God's sovereign rule (11–13), goodness will triumph and evil will be abolished; this consummation, to which we look forward in the Lord's Prayer, is promised in v. 20.

Meditation: 'Thy will be done on earth, even as it is in heaven.' When I say these words, how can I help on the fulfilment of my prayer?

7: 'Thou alone art the Lord'
Isaiah 37.8–38

Hezekiah, a descendant of David, sat on the throne of David 300 years after his great ancestor, and governed a sadly diminished kingdom. True, Hezekiah himself 'did what was right in the eyes of the LORD, according to all that David his father had done' (2 Kings 18.3), but his predecessor Ahaz had foolishly mortgaged the independence of Judah to the Assyrians, and now the Assyrians decided to foreclose and make Judah a province of their empire. What could Hezekiah do? He might trust in the God of his fathers, but could the God of his fathers help him against the Assyrians? The Assyrians themselves laughed at the idea. In their experience, the fortunes of national deities waxed and waned with the fortunes of the nations which worshipped them. 'Where are the gods of Hamath and Arpad?' asked the Assyrian envoy (Isa. 36.19). A pertinent question: where, indeed, are they? They vanished when the independence of Hamath and Arpad vanished before the Assyrian onslaught. And where is the God of Israel? In the Assyrians' eyes He was just another of those petty deities worshipped by the puny states of Western Asia: He would vanish before their onslaught as those others had done. But the Assyrian Empire has vanished, like many another empire since; the God of Israel survives. Why? Because He is 'the *living* God' (17). We know this today, but how could Hezekiah know it at that time of fearful danger?

11

When the Assyrian king, called aside to deal with a diversionary tactic on his Egyptian frontier, sent Hezekiah an intimidating letter (10–13), Hezekiah placed it before the Lord and poured out his soul in prayer. The gods of the other nations could not help their worshippers because 'they were no gods, but the work of men's hands' (19)—or the projections of their minds. But the God of Israel was different: He was the Creator of the universe, God not of Israel only but 'of all the kingdoms of the earth' (16); and Hezekiah entreats Him to manifest His delivering power 'that all the kingdoms of the earth may know that thou alone art the LORD' (20). Perhaps it took this crisis to bring this truth home to Hezekiah in a practical way. The existence of the other gods depended on their worshippers; with the God of Israel it was the other way round. His people's existence depended on Him, as it still does. Through God's spokesman Isaiah, Hezekiah received the assurance that his prayer was heard; and confirmation followed swiftly with the destruction of the Assyrian army by no human sword (Isa. 37.36).

Meditation: The Living One still says to His people: 'Because I live, you will live also' (John 14.19).

Questions and themes for study and discussion on Studies 1–7

1. The very concept of God as King is unacceptable to many today because of its 'outmoded' connotation of authority. How does this affect our presentation of the biblical teaching about God's kingship?

2. Consider the whole principle of a 'chosen people'. What does it tell us about the nature of God and the nature of man?

3. What false gods in our society offer themselves as rivals to the sovereign claims of the living and true God?

4. Is there any sense in which a country, a city or a building today can be regarded in some special way as a dwelling place of God?

5. Isaiah assured Hezekiah that the Assyrian king would not enter Jerusalem (Isa. 37.33–35), and was proved a true prophet. When others gave Zedekiah in his day the same assurance with regard to the Babylonian king, they were denounced as false prophets (Jer. 28.15; cf. 32.3). Wherein did the difference lie?

12

TWO

Old Testament Prophecies of a Future Kingdom

8: 'The kingdom shall be the Lord's'
Numbers 24.10–19; Obadiah 15–21

Balaam, the Mesopotamian seer, divinely compelled to bless Israel when the Moabite king had hired him to curse them, is carried on by the Spirit of prophecy to tell that king what Israel will do to his people 'in the latter days' (14). Verses 15 and 16 contain a vivid description of the ecstasy of inspiration in which the shape of things to come appears before the seer's vision. The 'star out of Jacob' and 'sceptre out of Israel' (17) are in synonymous parallelism; so both refer to the same person. In the first instance, the reference is to David, who crushed Moab (2 Sam. 8.2), made Edom tributary (2 Sam. 8.13 f.) and imposed his rule over other neighbouring nations.

When David's successors grew weak, those nations regained their independence, and some of them, especially Edom, became thorns in Judah's side. Obadiah in particular denounces the Edomites' unbrotherly conduct when they gloated over the destruction of Jerusalem by the Chaldeans (Obad. 12 f.; cf. Psa. 137.7) and occupied the cross-roads so as to cut off the Jewish fugitives' way of escape (Obad. 14). One day, he declares, the roles will be reversed; Edom will disappear while the dispersed Jews will be restored and regain sovereignty over all the territories which had witnessed their distress.

Balaam's prophecy about the star and sceptre was interpreted in the Qumran community, the people of the Dead Sea Scrolls, as referring to the expected Messiah of David's line, and this interpretation became standard in the Christian Church. The prophecy is not expressly quoted in the New Testament, but there may be an echo of it in Jesus' description as 'the root and the offspring of David, the bright morning star' in Rev. 22.16. And appropriately so: Jesus is the One in whom these ancient oracles of sovereignty are fulfilled. *How* they are fulfilled is shown in James's speech to the Council of Jerusalem in Acts 15. 15–18, where the promise of Amos 9.11 f., that the house of

David will 'possess the remnant of Edom' is seen to be realized in the world-wide Christian mission, by which the Gentiles who are called by the name of the God of Israel are brought to bow in allegiance to great David's greater Son. Not by military conquest, as in David's day, but by the message of redeeming grace, is the Kingdom of Christ established.

Thought: The best way to destroy enemies is to turn them into friends. This is so often God's way.

9: 'All nations call him blessed'

Psalm 72

Psalm 72 belongs to the group commonly called 'Royal Psalms', which have as their distinctive feature the relation between God and His Anointed. The present psalm might be described as a prayer for the Son of David. Verse 1 is a prayer in all our versions, and the idiom of prayer continues throughout the psalm in the RSV and NEB, although the older English versions render vs. 2–17 as statements in the future indicative. Verses 18 and 19 constitute the doxology appended to Book II of the Psalter (Pss. 42–72)—a doxology which comes most fittingly at the end of this particular psalm. Verse 20 is a note marking the end of one of the smaller and earlier collections incorporated into the Psalter.

The psalm was suitable for the king's enthronement, and may have been repeated at an annual celebration of his kingship. That some of the language surpasses the normal bounds of poetic hyperbole, if it relates to any of the historical kings who sat on David's throne, was realized already in Old Testament times. Thus in Zech. 9.10 the words of v. 8 are taken up and applied to the King who comes to Zion 'humble and riding on an ass'—and we know who that King is (cf. Matt. 21.4 f.; John 12.15). It is not surprising, then, that both Jewish and Christian commentators saw in this psalm a reference to the coming Messiah. The conditions of righteousness, peace and prosperity for which prayer is here made remained but an ideal while the house of David reigned in Jerusalem; their fulfilment awaits the day when every knee bends in Jesus' name and every tongue confesses Him as Lord (Phil. 2.10 f.). With this interpretation the psalm has passed into English hymnody in two great para-

14

phrases—Isaac Watts' 'Jesus shall reign' and James Montgomery's 'Hail to the Lord's Anointed'.

Our previous studies have declared the certainty and perpetuity of God's Kingship; now we see more clearly the features of Him through whom God's Kingship is mediated to men—features which recur in God's introduction of His Servant in Isa. 42.1–4. Nearly fifty years ago a well-known Russian Christian, Vladimir Martzinkovsky, asked the then Chief Rabbi of Jerusalem what kind of person he expected the Messiah to be. The Chief Rabbi replied with a glowing word-picture, based largely on the language of Psa. 72. 'Now,' said his visitor, 'I should like to ask you one more question: in what respect does the person you have described differ from Jesus of Nazareth?' 'Please,' was the reply, 'let us not discuss that subject.'

Thought: The psalmist emphasizes the King's universal sway in v. 10 by mentioning lands which were distant from his perspective. Perhaps we could say: 'May the rulers of Moscow and Peking render Him tribute, may the rulers of Cairo and Calcutta bring gifts.' But how would believers in Moscow and Peking express the same sentiments?

10: 'A priest for ever'

Psalm 110

Here again our attention is directed particularly to the king himself. Like Psa. 72, this also is one of the 'Royal Psalms'. The psalmist, addressing the king by the Spirit of prophecy, assures him of divine aid in gaining victory over his enemies. But we should concentrate chiefly on the two oracles quoted by the psalmist—the divine invitation of v. 1 and the divine oath of v. 4. David and his successors were kings of Israel and Judah, but in Jerusalem they were also, by right of conquest, heirs to the ancient dynasty of priest-kings of which Melchizedek (Gen. 14.18–20) was the most illustrious member. Psa. 110, like Psa. 72, may have figured in enthronement ceremonies, but more important for our purpose is its New Testament application. Especially important is our Lord's appropriation of the oracle of v. 1 in His reply to the high priest at His trial: 'you will see the Son of man sitting at the right hand of power' (Mark 14.62). No wonder, then, that this oracle was adduced so frequently in

15

the early apostolic preaching as a leading 'testimony' for God's exaltation of Christ after His humiliation at the hands of men: this is the source of the traditional credal affirmation that Christ 'sitteth on the right hand of God the Father Almighty'. We should consider Peter's quotation of v. 1 on the day of Pentecost (Acts 2.34–36), from which it is plain also that it provided conclusive authority for giving to the exalted Christ the supreme title 'Lord'.

While this use of v. 1 pervades the New Testament, it is only the writer to the Hebrews who expressly applies v. 4 to Jesus. This further application followed inevitably: if Jesus is the One called to share the throne of God, He must also be the One acclaimed as 'a priest for ever'. This insight had been anticipated by Paul (and probably by others), as appears from Rom. 8.34, where 'Christ Jesus, who died' is 'at the right hand of God' and 'intercedes for us'; but it is in Hebrews that it is statedly founded on Psa. 110.4. At the right hand of God the enthroned Son 'holds his priesthood permanently' on the basis of His unique and perfect self-sacrifice, and 'is able for all time to save those who draw near to God through him, since he always lives to make intercession for them' (Heb. 7.24 f.).

The enemies who are to become Messiah's footstool are shown in 1 Cor. 15.25–28 to be hostile spiritual forces, including (finally) death; the language of slaughter in Psa. 110.6, literally applicable to the circumstances of David's day, must be appropriately transmuted to denote the destruction of those spiritual forces.

Meditation: 'David himself calls him Lord; so how is he his Son?' (*Mark* 12.37).

11: 'The City of the Lord'
Isaiah 60

The preceding chapters of Isaiah have celebrated the restoration of Jerusalem and the return of her children from exile: now the city herself, personified as a queen, is addressed. The divine glory which was seen in Solomon's temple (1 Kings 8.10 f.) now invests the whole city with a light greater than that of sun or moon; she is God's dwelling-place on earth, the city of the great King (Psa. 48.2), and distant nations come to bring Him their tribute of worship.

But we shall look in vain for an occasion when this vision was realized in post-exilic Jerusalem. To see the place which it occupied in the complete biblical view of the Kingdom of God, we must recall that in the New Testament the restoration celebrated in Isa. 40–66 is applied to the gospel age. The wise men's visit to pay homage to the infant King of the Jews (Matt. 2.1–12) was early recognized (probably by the Evangelist himself) as the fulfilment of Isa. 60.3. But the New Testament passage which draws most fully on Isa. 60 is the description of the new Jerusalem in Rev. 21.10–22.5; it is here that we find the *Christian* interpretation of Isa. 60. The new Jerusalem is the perfected Church, the glorified city of God, whose presence on earth means the healing of the nations. One after another of the motifs of Isa. 60 recur in John's description. Still the nations come to the light of the city and their kings bring their glory into it; but to the glory of God, which is its true light, is now added the glory of Christ: 'its lamp is the Lamb' (Rev. 21.23). For between the call to prepare the Lord's way in the wilderness (Isa. 40.3), applied in the New Testament to John the Baptist's ministry, and the vision of the latter-day glory of the Church in Isa. 60, comes the passion and triumph of the Servant of the Lord, 'like a lamb that is led to the slaughter' (Isa. 52.13–53.12).

Meditation: The city of God is the community of the elect, not in the sense that outside of it all are consigned to perdition, but that through it many enjoy divine blessing.

12: 'It shall stand for ever'

Daniel 2.1–3, 25–49

Daniel surpasses all other Old Testament books in the sweep of its historical perspective. In its visions the ultimate secrets of history are divulged. World-empires rise through the military and political power of a Nebuchadnezzar, a Cyrus, an Alexander. The founder of the empire is apt to exaggerate his achievement and to imagine that his structure will last for ever—or at least for a thousand years. We remember such a millennial boast being voiced for a European régime between thirty and forty years ago; it lasted twelve years. Britain has witnessed the fulfilment of a prophecy made by one of her own poets in 1897, at the peak of her imperial might:

17

'Lo, all our pomp of yesterday
Is one with Nineveh and Tyre!'

It is difficult for founders of empires to view themselves in the perspective of history. Daniel, however, shows Nebuchadnezzar and his successors how to view themselves and their achievements from the perspective of God's purpose. It is the Most High who, in His wisdom, 'rules the kingdom of men, and gives it to whom he will, and sets over it the lowliest of men' (Dan. 4.17).

The independence of Israel and Judah had been lost; David's throne lay unoccupied, but the God of Israel had not abdicated His universal sovereignty. He not only overrules the course of human affairs but is able, when He chooses, to reveal the mystery of His purpose.

Of the four metals making up the image which Nebuchadnezzar saw in his dream only one is expressly identified in the interpretation: Nebuchadnezzar himself is the head of gold (38). There is more doubt about the precise identity of the others than those brought up in one school of interpretation might imagine. No matter: the important feature is the stone cut out without hands, which pulverizes the great image of secular imperialism and replaces it by God's eternal Kingdom.

Meditation:

> *The Kingdoms of the Earth go by*
> *In purple and in gold;*
> *They rise, they triumph, and they die,*
> *And all their tale is told.*

> *One Kingdom only is divine,*
> *One banner triumphs still;*
> *Its King a servant, and its sign*
> *A gibbet on a hill.*

(G. F. Bradby)

13: 'One like a son of man'

Daniel 7

As Daniel in ch. 2 explained Nebuchadnezzar's dream, so now an interpreting angel explains Daniel's dream. The patterns of the two dreams are parallel: the four beasts in ch. 7 correspond to the four metals in ch. 2 and the 'one like a son of man' in ch. **7** corresponds to the stone in ch. **2**. But in ch. **7** the four empires are passed over rapidly, until we come to the fourth beast with its 'little horn' (historically Antiochus Epiphanes) warring against the saints. Then our attention is concentrated on the world judgement executed by the Ancient of Days and the bestowal of universal and eternal sovereignty on 'one like a son of man' (13)—a human figure in contrast to the monsters that preceded him. If in the dream the kingdom is given to him, in the interpretation it is given to 'the saints of the Most High' (18). There is no chapter of the Old Testament (with the possible exception of Isa. **53**) which has so profoundly influenced the New Testament as this. When Jesus appeared in Galilee and announced 'The time is fulfilled, and the kingdom of God is at hand' (Mark **1**.15), He echoed v. 22: 'the time came when the saints received the kingdom.' Throughout the Gospels He associates the Kingdom of God closely with the Son of Man, and when at last He is challenged to reveal His identity before the Sanhedrin He replies: 'you will see the Son of man ... coming with the clouds of heaven' (Mark **14**.62). As the Kingdom when first proclaimed is subject to limitations but will at length come 'with power' (Mark **9**.1), so the Son of Man must first suffer and be rejected before He is manifested in glory (Mark **8**.31; **13**.26). The dominion is imparted primarily to Him, but He shares it with His followers: 'Fear not, little flock, for it is your Father's good pleasure to give you the kingdom' (Luke **12**.32). Thus the individual figure in Daniel's vision (13) and the community in its interpretation (18) have their closely associated counterparts in the New Testament fulfilment.

Meditation: 'He who conquers, I will grant him to sit with me on my throne, as I myself conquered and sat down with my Father on his throne' (Rev. 3.21).

Questions and themes for study and discussion on Studies 8-13

1. Consider the way in which Old Testament language of military conquest and destruction (e.g. Num. **24**.17; Psa. **110**.5, 6) has come to be applied to the victorious advance of the gospel. Can this use of such language be justified by scriptural precedent?

2. Psa. **72**, which in our older versions (e.g. AV [KJV]) appears to be a prophecy of the rule of the Lord's Anointed,

19

is rendered in the RSV as a prayer for his prosperity. Does this make a material difference to its messianic interpretation?

3. Do you think the traditional Christian interpretation of Isa. 60 with reference to the Church is well founded? Could it have a valid meaning for a Jew today in reference, say, to the State of Israel?

4. 'The history of the world is the judgement of the world' (Schiller). Consider the truth of this epigram (a) in the light of Daniel's visions, and (b) in the light of world events in our own lifetime.

THREE

The Faithful Remnant in the Old Testament

14: Not 'I only'—but Seven Thousand
1 Kings 19. 1–18

The doctrine of the faithful remnant in the Old Testament is specially associated with the prophet Isaiah. In an earlier study we have seen how he recognized the hope of the future to be bound up with the survival of a remnant (Isa. 37.31 f.). But the idea did not originate with him. God was always King in Israel, but effectively so where His kingship was acknowledged. There was a widespread repudiation of His kingship in the northern realm during Ahab's reign, thanks largely to Ahab's marriage alliance with the Phoenician princess Jezebel. One man protested publicly against the prevalent trend, challenging court and people alike for their Baal worship, and because he 'stood up and spoke for God' the rot was stopped. But Elijah imagined mistakenly that he was the only man in Israel not to participate in the national apostasy. His mistake was pointed out to him by God.

Only by judgement would the apostasy be purged, and Elijah was charged to commission the three executors of judgement—Hazael, king of Syria, whose armies would carry fire and sword to the farthest limits of Israel; Jehu, who would wipe out the house of Ahab; and Elisha, Elijah's own successor in the prophetic office. To what a low condition Israel was actually reduced when these had fulfilled their ministry is amply recorded in the sequel: 'the affliction of Israel was very bitter, . . . and there was none to help Israel' (2 Kings 14.26). But, the narrator goes on, 'the LORD had not said that he would blot out the name of Israel from under heaven' (2 Kings 14.27)—no indeed: at the end of His ominous utterance to Elijah He added, 'Yet I will leave seven thousand in Israel, all the knees that have not bowed to Baal' (18). In them the hope of Israel's survival was embodied. In Rom. 11.2–5 Paul points out that this is not an isolated instance; rather it exemplifies a recurring pattern of divine action: 'So too at the present time there is a remnant, chosen by grace' (Rom. 11.5). The fact that he and others belonged to that

21

'remnant' of Jews who confessed Jesus as Lord was a guarantee that one day 'all Israel' would be saved (Rom. **11**.26).

Meditation:
> *When stronger souls their faith forsook,*
> *And lulled in worldly hellish peace,*
> *Leaped desperate from their guardian Rock,*
> *And headlong plunged in sin's abyss,*
> *Thy power was in our weakness shown,*
> *And still it keeps our souls Thine own.*

(C. Wesley)

15: 'My eyes have seen the King'

Isaiah 6

It is with Isaiah, as we have seen, that the Old Testament remnant doctrine is chiefly connected. It is striking how many of the dominant notes of his ministry are struck in this inaugural vision. The seraphs' insistence on the holiness of God, for example, may have influenced Isaiah's repeated designation of Him as 'the Holy One of Israel'. But the note which concerns us at present is that of God's kingship.

Uzziah had been king of Judah for half a century—so long that only a few of his oldest subjects could recall a time when he had not been king. His death marked the end of an era. A symbol of permanence and stability disappeared when he died. The future was uncertain. At home, the mercantile prosperity of Uzziah's reign was established on a foundation of economic oppression—a state of affairs which some perhaps saw mirrored in the leprosy from which the king suffered in his closing years. Abroad, events were taking an unpromising turn: the great power of Assyria to the north-east was flexing its muscles in a way that augured ill for the small states in the west. In such an atmosphere of uncertainty Isaiah saw this vision of the Divine King, enthroned eternally, maintaining His sovereignty over the whole earth. The Lord of hosts was no mere *symbol* of stability; He was the source and ground of all stability, for those who put their trust in Him. 'If you will not believe, surely you shall not be established' (Isa. 7.9).

Here, then, in the presence of 'the King, the Lord of hosts' (5), young Isaiah received three things: the conviction of his unfitness to stand before God or speak for Him, the bestowal by divine grace of the fitness which he lacked, and the call to go and speak for God. He was not to suppose that the people would pay any heed to his message: the more he spoke, the more unreceptive they would become. The forecast of their failure to respond (9 f.) is taken up repeatedly in the New Testament as a prophecy of the unbelief which greeted Jesus' ministry (e.g. Mark **4**.12; John **12**.40; Acts **28**.26 f.). Exile and desolation would follow (11 f.), but though the oak of Israel was cut down to the merest stump, from that stump—'the holy seed', the faithful remnant—new life could spring forth (13, cf. **11**.1).

Thought: 'Here am I! Send me,' said Isaiah, and he was sent with a message for his own city. It is sometimes more difficult to take God's message across the street than across the sea.

16: 'To the teaching and to the testimony!'
Isaiah 8.11–22

Isaiah carried his message to King Ahaz, Uzziah's grandson, but Ahaz had already launched a short-sighted policy which was incompatible with that message and mortgaged the hope of Israel (7.1–17). Isaiah then placarded his message publicly before the people of Jerusalem, but they too preferred their ruler's policy of alliance with Assyria, an alliance which threatened to dethrone God from His people's worship (8.1–8). Therefore they would have their fill of the allies in whom they trusted, but as invaders, not as allies—and where would they turn for refuge then? The faithful remnant had as its watchword the name of the virgin's Son, 'God is with us' (8.10, cf. 7.14); but what hope was there for those who 'despised the Holy One of Israel' (1.4)?

To those who put their trust in Him God would be a sanctuary, a rock of refuge amid the swirling flood-waters of foreign invasion; but those who refused to trust in Him would find themselves dashed to pieces against that rock by those flood-waters. What was a rock of refuge to believers would be a 'rock of stumbling' to unbelievers (13–15). Here too is a motif which recurs in a similar situation in the New Testament (cf. Rom. **9**.32 f.; 1 Pet. **2**.8).

Having delivered his message of warning, Isaiah sealed it up and committed it for safe-keeping to his disciples (16). Even if he did not live to see its fulfilment, when that fulfilment came the seal could be broken and it would be known that what he had spoken was the Word of God. Isaiah's disciples may well have formed a nucleus for the faithful remnant, as did Isaiah himself and his two sons with their significant names, summarizing leading themes of their father's ministry—'A remnant will return' and 'Hasten booty, speed spoil'. They in the meantime would be living 'signs' reminding the people of the divine warning which they had ignored (18). The hidden God (17) was still the living God. Those who forsook Him would have recourse in their impending distress to mediums and wizards, and would get no help from them (19). The chapter ends (20-22) with a fearful picture of social disintegration and eviction—and all because they chose not to listen to their true King, thinking that they knew better. But a remnant did return.

Meditation: Consider the context of the quotation of parts of vs. 17 and 18 in Heb. 2.13. What was there about Isaiah in this situation which presented an analogy to Christ?

17: 'Those who feared the Lord'

Malachi 3.13–4.5

Israel and Judah went into exile, as the prophets foretold, and a remnant returned. They were conscious of their responsibility not to compromise the true knowledge of God again, as their forefathers had done, and when they started to restore the temple they refused the co-operation of their kinsfolk who had remained behind in Palestine. Under the guidance of Ezra and Nehemiah they reaffirmed their allegiance to God, covenanting to obey His law and not practise intermarriage with 'the peoples of the lands' (Neh. 9.38 –10.31.). But, as in earlier days, it was easier to undertake such a covenant than to keep it. They grew lax in their attention to details which they had specifically mentioned. in their covenant oath, and complained that obedience to God's law brought no material advantages. Why should they not imitate the life-style of their irreligious neighbours?

In this situation a new remnant began to take shape, comprising 'those who feared the LORD' (3.16). Those people met informally for mutual encouragement. Malachi pictures a record of their names and actions being kept in heaven, like the book at the Persian court in which benefactors and their services were registered (Esth. 2.23; 6.1). On the day of divine visitation they would receive their reward (3.17; 4.2), while the ungodly would undergo judgement (4.1, 3). This faithful remnant, the 'pious folk' (*hasidim*), as they came to be called, bore the brunt of the persecution when in 168 B.C. and the following years Antiochus Epiphanes tried to abolish the Jewish religion and way of life. From their ranks, a generation or so later, came the Qumran 'volunteers for holiness'; from their ranks, too, came the godly community of the 'quiet in the land' into which John the Baptist and our Lord were born—men and women who were 'looking for the consolation of Israel' (Luke 2.25) and recognized in the infant Jesus the fulfilment of their hopes. Zechariah and Elizabeth, Joseph and Mary, Simeon and Anna, whom we meet in Luke's nativity narrative, all belonged to this noble succession.

Meditation: Consider how the theme of Malachi 4 is echoed in the ministry of John the Baptist, and assess the significance of Luke 1.17 in this regard.

18: The true Israel

Romans 2.25–29; 9.1–29

Once the truth was grasped that natural descent from the patriarchs was not enough to win God's approval, but that obedience to His will was essential, the next step (and a long one) was the realization that, if obedience to God's will was present, descent from the patriarchs was a matter of indifference. John the Baptist, as our next study will show, hovered on the brink of this realization (Matt. 3.9). But Paul embraces it without reserve. A Jew is a member of the tribe of Judah. But Judah means 'praise'; the true Jew therefore is the man who receives praise from God, regardless of his parentage. Even in Old Testament times God had taught His people through Moses and Jeremiah that the circumcision which He required was the 'circumcision of the heart'; inward purity (Deut. 10.16; 30.6; Jer. 4.4). This circumcision was available to Gentiles as readily as to Jews: 'we are the true circumcision, who worship God in spirit, and glory in Christ Jesus' (Phil. 3.3). Or, as it is put in Rom. 9.6–8, it is the children of promise, whether Gentiles or Jews, who are the true Israel. Here Paul applies Isaiah's message of the faithful remnant to a new situation which expresses definitely a principle manifested throughout Israel's history. Abraham had several sons, but it was through Isaac alone that the line of promise was traced; accordingly Abraham's true

25

children are those who inherit the promise made to faith. Similarly, Isaac had two sons, but it was on Jacob, not Esau, that the divine choice fell—and that apart from any question of merit in the one or the other. And if the pattern be extended to cover the Gentile world, Pharaoh illustrates God's power to overrule men's unbelief and obstinacy for the accomplishment of His purpose.

Again, already in Old Testament times it was seen how God could bring into the circle of His blessing those who had once been excluded from it. In Hosea's day God acted thus within the frontiers of Israel (25 f.), but now the Gentile mission showed the same principle at work beyond those frontiers. Those who formerly were not God's people were now in large numbers being acknowledged by Him as His sons. The remnant survives not only for its own sake, but as an earnest of blessing on a far wider scale.

Thought: Consider Rom. 2.26, 27. How far can we say that there are today people who are Christians in fact though not in name, whose lives condemn those who are Christians in name but not in fact?

Questions and themes for study and discussion on Studies 14-18

1. How is the Old Testament teaching about the 'remnant'—a saved remnant which becomes a saving remnant—taken up and applied in the New Testament?

2. Sometimes today we come across small groups of godly people who feel themselves to be a faithful remnant amid the surrounding apostasy. Does the Bible give any countenance to this idea in the Christian age? Do such people present a counterpart to those of Mal. 3.16? Or might God have to tell them, as He told Elijah, that there are 7,000 times as many who have remained faithful to Him?

3. 'He is not a real Jew who is one outwardly' (Rom. 2.28). We should agree that this could be paralleled with a statement that 'he is not a real Christian who is one outwardly'— but how should we then go on and say what the marks of a real Christian are?

FOUR

The Kingdom of God in the New Testament

19: 'The kingdom of heaven is at hand'

Matthew 3; 4.12–17

In Mal. 4.5, as we saw, God promised to send Elijah the prophet 'before the great and terrible day of the LORD comes'. And now, in the spirit and power of Elijah, John the Baptist inaugurates his ministry, calling on Israel to repent in view of the approach of the Kingdom of heaven, and to make ready for the imminent advent of the Coming One. The ministry of the Coming One will mean the cutting down of every fruitless tree, the gathering of the wheat and the burning of the chaff. (We should observe that the expression 'the kingdom of heaven' is peculiar to Matthew's Gospel; it is completely synonymous with 'the kingdom of God'.)

It was useless for John's hearers to assert that they were Abraham's descendants, as though God were concerned about pedigrees. God, if He so wished, could create children of Abraham out of the stones on the ground. What God wanted was heart-devotion and righteous living. These were the qualities that marked His Kingdom, and they would be acceptable to Him apart from any question of natural parentage.

And now there appears One who embodies those qualities in perfection and is therefore the very embodiment of the Kingdom. John knew this well, and therefore demurred at the invitation to administer the baptism of repentance to One who had no need to repent (14). Jesus' reply, 'We do well to conform in this way with all that God requires' (15, NEB), sums up the essence of life in the Kingdom of God and His own single-minded ambition—as the heavenly voice acknowledges (17).

Jesus is endowed with the Spirit that He may baptize with the Spirit, but in a way that transcended what John could envisage. When, after John's imprisonment, He took up His Galilean ministry, He repeated John's announcement (4.17, cf. 3.2), but in a new sense. For John the Kingdom lay in the future; with Jesus, it is present—not yet in power, indeed, but none the less really.

27

Question: *Why did Jesus insist on receiving John's baptism, seeing it was a baptism of repentance?*

20: The Law of the Kingdom

Matthew 5

The Sermon on the Mount (Matt. 5–7) may be called the law of the Kingdom of God, if we use the word 'law' in a more general sense than when we speak of the law of Sinai. The beatitudes (3–10) certainly could not be enforced by Act of Parliament. They sum up the character of the true heir of the Kingdom, the character displayed in Jesus Himself. In a world not governed by the principles of the Kingdom, those who manifest such qualities are almost bound to be 'persecuted for righteousness' sake' (10). But they are the people who ought to be congratulated; the future belongs to them. The beatitudes are more subversive of established priorities than the Baptist's fiery denunciations: it is only their familiarity that blinds Christians to their revolutionary tenor.

Jesus does not abrogate the ethical demands of the Old Testament; He brings them to completion and extends their scope. He applies them not only to overt deeds or words but to the inner springs of action—angry thoughts, illicit desires. How quickly His 'hard sayings' were modified is shown by the early insertion of the phrase 'without a cause' into the clause: 'every one who is angry with his brother' (22). The law permitting divorce is revised (31, 32); it is unthinkable that such a breach should occur within the fellowship of the Kingdom. The law forbidding false swearing is transformed into a prohibition of all swearing (33–37); in the fellowship of the Kingdom a plain statement should be evidence enough. The law of retaliation (Exod. 21.23 ff.), which once marked an advance on the earlier blood-feud, is now replaced by the law of non-retaliation (38–42). Clearly, law and order would collapse if a secular state attempted to live by this law; yet it is the natural way of life for citizens of that Kingdom whose King provides the supreme example of non-retaliation. The 'undistinguishing regard' with which God bestows His blessings lays down the pattern which His children must reproduce. Paul caught the spirit of these words perfectly when he summed them up in the admonition: 'Do not be overcome by evil but overcome evil with good' (Rom. 12.21).

28

If men have found the Ten Commandments difficult, what hope is there, apart from divine grace, of living according to the Sermon on the Mount?

Meditation:

> *To run and work the law commands,*
> *Yet gives me neither feet nor hands;*
> *But better news the gospel brings:*
> *It bids me fly, and gives me wings.*

21: 'Seek first his kingdom'

Matthew 6

The 'piety' of v. 1 covers such religious practices as almsgiving (2–4), prayer (5–15) and fasting (16–18). These were largely voluntary, so there was a tendency to suppose that by assiduous attention to them one might acquire merit before God, as well as a good reputation among men. Jesus insists that only as such activity is directed towards God, with no self-regarding motive, is it true piety. The Lord's Prayer (9–13) is primarily a prayer for children of the Kingdom; it serves also as a concise but comprehensive summary of the main emphases of the message of the Kingdom—the Fatherhood of God, the presence of His Kingdom when His name is sanctified by the doing of His will, His provision for daily need, His forgiving grace, His imparting strength to endure testing without loss of faith, His protection against the power of evil.

The carefree and trustful attitude to life inculcated in vs. 19–34 was difficult enough to cultivate in the situation of Jesus' contemporaries, for many of whom constant back-breaking toil was necessary to keep themselves and their families living at subsistence level. We might argue that the complexities of western life today make it even more difficult for us. Is it practicable to exercise such childlike trust in God that we have no anxiety for tomorrow and make no provision for the future? Do we not tend to regard people who put this teaching into literal practice as a trifle naïve? Are they not opting out of their social obligations? Not really; social obligations are bound up with love to one's neighbour. The difficulty is that, whereas Jesus speaks throughout in terms of personal relationships, modern society is so institutionalized that the interests of persons as persons, even in a welfare state, can be subordinated to the processes of social engineering. The followers of Jesus must be on their guard against such conformity to the spirit of the age, and must treat persons as persons.

Meditation: Is it possible for Christians today to fulfil their religious exercises as so many rules to be kept, and to imagine that, if they perform them regularly, God will be better pleased with them than with others whose record in such matters is deplorably lax?

22: 'The way is hard'

Matthew 7

It is not a judicious discernment but a censorious spirit that is forbidden in vs. 1–5. The teaching about prayer in 6.5–15 is reinforced by the words of encouragement in vs. 7–11. True children of the Kingdom have that implicit trust in God which ordinary children have in their earthly fathers. The law of the Kingdom is summed up in one sentence in v. 12, the Golden Rule. Jesus was not the first teacher in Israel to formulate this rule, though earlier formulations expressed it negatively: 'what you hate, do not to any one' (Tobit 4.15).

The Kingdom of God and eternal life in the Gospels are largely interchangeable terms: to enter the one is to enter the other. The way 'that leads to life' (14) is the way into the Kingdom. No one drifts into it inadvertently; it must be chosen deliberately, resolutely and with due recognition of what it involves in the way of self-denial and sacrifice. The children of the Kingdom are recognized not by their pious phraseology but by the character of the lives they live, just as the nature of a tree is shown by the fruit it produces (16–23). A life founded on the teaching of Jesus, more especially on His teaching in the Sermon on the Mount, is a well-founded life; it will stand in the day of adversity. But a life which ignores His teaching is unstable and liable to collapse.

It is so easy to pay lip-service to all this, to assume that it is self-evidently so. But when we consider how far the principles of the Sermon on the Mount underlie our personal and community life as Christians, not to speak of life organized on a national or international plane, the gap between profession and reality becomes too painfully apparent. 'The teaching of Jesus is difficult and unacceptable because it runs counter to those elements in human nature which the twentieth century has in common with the first—such things as laziness, greed, the love of pleasure, the instinct to hit back and the like. The teaching as a whole shows that Jesus was well aware of this and recognized that here and nowhere else lay the obstacle that had to be surmounted' (T. W. Manson).

Question: Can a Christian ever be in a situation when he cannot practise the Golden Rule? If so, should he ever be in such a situation?

23: Parables of the Kingdom

Matthew 13

This chapter brings together seven parables in which various aspects of Jesus' message of the Kingdom are graphically portrayed. Three of them are parables of growth—the parables of the sower (3-9, 18-23), of the weeds or 'tares' (24-30, 36-43) and of the mustard seed (31 f.). The first depicts the good news of the Kingdom broadcast indiscriminately to receptive and non-receptive hearers alike; if some refuse or ignore it, that does not make its proclamation fruitless, for the abundant fruit that it produces in the lives of those who welcome it makes the task of proclaiming it incomparably worth while. The parable of the weeds envisages a situation in which, for the time being, true sons of the Kingdom and counterfeit disciples are so intermingled that they cannot be sorted out: premature weeding out is discouraged because it requires a degree of spiritual discernment which few possess. Better let both grow together until the fruit (or lack of it) appears, and then the two crops will be seen for what they are. The parable of the mustard seed reminds us that great enterprises may have very small and modest beginnings. So it was with the Kingdom: in Jesus' day the number of His genuine followers was small indeed, but by the time Matthew wrote his Gospel it had increased beyond computation. The parable of the leaven (33) is to the same effect: as the leaven 'hidden' in the meal works unobtrusively, so Jesus in His ministry then was launching the Kingdom of heaven on earth—'Now let it work!'

31

The parables of the hidden treasure (44) and the costly pearl (45 f.) are companion pieces which stress the paramount value of the Kingdom. Let a man sacrifice everything he has rather than miss this—because, of course, the Kingdom is life itself. The parable of the dragnet (47–50) has much the same point as the parable of the weeds, except that the emphasis is entirely on the separation at the final judgement, not on any antecedent process.

Meditation: 'He who has ears, let him hear' (9). Consider the case of those who have ears but will not hear (14, 15).

24: The Fellowship of the Kingdom

Matthew 18

It was difficult for Jesus' disciples not to think of the Kingdom of heaven after the analogy of earthly kingdoms. In these, there was the king at the top, of course, but next to him there were privileged people who were looked up to and envied by ordinary folk. Who would those privileged people be in the Kingdom of heaven? The disciples naturally cast themselves in this role, but who, they wondered, would be chief among them? 'Never mind thinking of being chief', Jesus told them in effect; 'you won't even enter the Kingdom unless you execute a right-about-turn in your thinking and become as humble, trustful and unassuming as little children' (3).

This leads on to further sayings of Jesus about little ones, and then comes a central section in which the two themes of our present course of studies—Kingdom and Church—are brought together. Verses 15–20 introduce the subject of the fellowship of the Kingdom. This fellowship is enjoyed and manifested in the community of Jesus' followers which is here called the Church (17), the community of the two or three who are gathered together in Jesus' name (20). The simple community rules of this section assume a primitive stage of church life, but they embody a basic and permanent principle of Christian fellowship—it is Jesus' presence in the midst that makes that fellowship what it is.

Peter's question about the number of times he should be expected to show forgiveness (21) leads not only to the answer 'seventy times seven' (22) but to a further parable of the Kingdom, which elaborates the postscript to the Lord's Prayer in 6.14 f. Not only should God's forgiveness be reflected in His children's forgiveness of one another; it is conditional on their forgiveness of one another. Jesus says so plainly (35) and it is not for His disciples (meaning ourselves) to argue that He does not mean what He says. In this parable a man whose debt ran into millions was forgiven by his royal master, but then set the law in motion against a fellow-servant who owed him a relatively trifling sum. His pardon was revoked. But (we may imagine one of the disciples exclaiming) God wouldn't do a thing like that! 'O yes, He would,' Jesus replies—'and He will.' This does not contradict the gospel of grace; it is a corollary of that gospel. True children of the Kingdom will show their Father's forgiving spirit; those who do not have no place in His Kingdom.

Thought: If Jesus, presence in the midst constitutes the fellowship of the Kingdom, no conduct inconsistent with His presence can be consistent with that fellowship.

25: Who Receives the Kingdom?

Luke 18.9–30

Luke's account of Jesus' requirements for entry into the Kingdom of God does not differ from Matthew's. Humility, childlikeness and self-denial are the marks of those who belong to it. The parable of the Pharisee and the tax collector (9–14) is not explicitly called a parable of the Kingdom, but it is one in essence. The Pharisee had much to thank God for, and in fact he did thank Him for it all; but to compare one's own piety advantageously with someone else's is no fit exercise in the presence of God, before whom we stand on one level, as sinners in need of His grace. The tax collector, having no acts of piety to enumerate, could but confess his sin and cast himself on God's mercy. Therefore, said Jesus, it was he who went home 'justified' (14).

The blessing of the children (15–17) is another incident which, like that of Matt. 18.1–4, gives Jesus occasion to affirm that the Kingdom is open only to those who display something of that transparent simplicity and dependence found in small children. 'It is children,' said one rabbi, 'who receive the presence of the Shekinah.'

33

The incident of the ruler (18–30) is important in several ways. For one thing, it shows that to 'inherit eternal life' (18) is to 'enter the kingdom of God' (24). For another, it shows how Jesus brought out the full implications of the Old Testament law of love to one's neighbour. To keep the letter of the individual commandments, as the ruler had done (21), is not enough; if I can do something to help another, and fail to do it, I have not kept the spirit of the law. An attachment to mere things is incompatible with the Kingdom of God, in which personal relations are all-important—especially incompatible when attachment to things takes precedence over love to one's neighbour. The more property we have, the more attached we tend to become to it. That is why Jesus emphasized the impossibility of a rich man's entering the Kingdom, unless the grace of God saves him from that attachment. This is such a hard saying that commentators have regularly tried to soften it—but our Lord knew the human nature He was dealing with and meant what He said. Those, however, who had abandoned the fancied security of temporal possessions for the sake of the Kingdom, would receive overwhelming compensation here and now, not to speak of eternal life in the new age.

Meditation: 'Verily, I say unto you, there is no man that hath invested in slum houses or government bonds or suburban real estate or blue-chip securities or stocks for Mammon's sake who shall not receive manifold more dividends in this present time, and in the years ahead, everlasting status' (Clarence Jordan).

26: The Kingdom Coming with Power
Acts 1.1–14

In Jesus' ministry the Kingdom of God was in process of inauguration. With His death and resurrection, followed by the descent of the Spirit, this process was completed. The Kingdom has now been inaugurated: in Jesus' words, it has 'come with power' (Mark 9.1). This Kingdom, according to Luke, was the subject of Jesus' instruction to His disciples when He appeared to them at intervals during the forty days between His resurrection and ascension. 'The Kingdom of God is conceived as coming in the events of the life, death, and resurrection of Jesus, and to proclaim these facts, in their proper setting, is to preach

34

the Gospel of the Kingdom of God' (C. H. Dodd). There remains the consummation of the Kingdom at the end of the age, but the consummation is but the outworking of the inauguration, and does not differ from it in character.

The disciples found it difficult even now to dissociate their understanding of the Kingdom from the national hope with which they had grown up. So when their risen Lord speaks of the imminent coming of the Spirit and of the 'power' which they will receive thereby, they think of Israel's political restoration. Had not this restoration been linked in Old Testament prophecy with God's bestowal of His Spirit on His people (Ezek. 36.26 f.; 37.14)? Instead of telling them that they are quite wrong, Jesus says rather that certain areas of knowledge are withheld from them. Only by experience of the Spirit's ministry in years to come would they learn what 'Israel' meant in terms of the new era into which they were entering. We today have the advantage of hindsight: in the light of the complete New Testament we know that the national hope of Old Testament times was transformed into something that transcended earlier aspirations. But the disciples at this early stage had not had the opportunity of reading Rom. 11.11–32; we need not imagine ourselves to be wiser than they because we have a fuller revelation of what was involved in the 'Christ-event'.

Question: 'This Jesus . . . will come in the same way as you saw him go' (11). What are the principal features which, according to the New Testament, His return has in common with His departure?

27: The Continuing Proclamation of the Kingdom of God

Acts 28.17–31

At the end of Acts, as at the beginning (1.3), the Kingdom of God is the major theme. What the risen Lord taught His disciples in Jerusalem is now proclaimed by Paul in the capital of the Gentile world. Philip in Samaria 'preached good news about the kingdom of God and the name of Jesus Christ' (8.12). Paul and Barnabas warned the believers of South Galatia that 'through many tribulations we must enter the kingdom of God' (14.22). Paul spent three months in the synagogue of Ephesus 'arguing and pleading about the Kingdom of God' (19.8) and continued for over two more years in that city 'preaching the kingdom' (20.25). (It is evident from a comparison of vs. 24 and

25 of Acts 20 that 'preaching the kingdom' is the same thing as 'to testify to the gospel of the grace of God'.) And now in Rome Paul is still found 'testifying to the kingdom of God' to the local Jewish leaders (23) and 'preaching the kingdom of God and teaching about the Lord Jesus Christ' unhindered to all and sundry in the city (31). 'Evidently on purpose are the two expressions combined in this final summary, in order to show that the preaching of the Kingdom and the preaching of Christ are one; that the original proclamation has now ceased, but that in Christ Jesus the thing proclaimed is no longer a vague and future hope, but a distinct and present fact. In the conjunction of these words the progress of doctrine appears. All is founded upon the old Jewish expectation of a Kingdom of God; but it is now explained how that expectation is fulfilled in the person of Jesus; and the account of its realization consists in the unfolding of the truth concerning him, "the things concerning Jesus". The manifestation of Christ being finished, the Kingdom is already begun. Those who receive *him* enter into *it*. Having overcome the sharpness of death, he has opened the Kingdom of heaven to all believers. Those, therefore, who were once to "tell no man that he was Christ", are now to make "all the house of Israel know assuredly that God hath made that same Jesus, whom they had crucified, both Lord and Christ"; yea, they are to proclaim that fact to every nation under heaven' (T. D. Bernard).

Meditation: Look back to Isa. **6.9**, *10 (Study* 15) *and consider the appositeness of these two verses to the gospel situation here and elsewhere in the New Testament.*

28: The Consummation of the Kingdom

1 Corinthians 15.20–28, 35–50

Before His death our Lord was conscious of limitations: 'I have a baptism to be baptized with,' He said, 'and how I am constrained until it is accomplished!' (Luke **12.50**). But with His death and triumph the full power of the Kingdom was unleashed. With Christ enthroned in glory, and His Spirit active on earth, nothing can stop its advance. In His exaltation the early Christians recognized the fulfilment of the oracle of Psa. **110.1**: 'Sit at my right hand, till I make your enemies your footstool.' But the only New Testament passage which clearly interprets these 'enemies' is 1 Cor. **15**.24–27. Here they are shown to be all the spiritual forces, the principalities and powers, which are opposed to 'the LORD and his anointed' (Psa. **2**.2). Christ must continue to reign until God has put them all beneath His feet (25). The annihilation of death, the last of these enemies, coincides with the resurrection of the people of Christ. In 2 Tim. **1**.10 Christ is described as already having 'abolished death and brought life and immortality to light through the gospel'. As His own resurrection carries with it the certainty of His people's resurrection (23), so His personal conquest of death carries with it the certainty of death's ultimate destruction. But this means the introduction of a new order of existence and the end of the kingship of Christ in the form in which it has been exercised hitherto. When He has completed the work of bringing the whole estranged creation back into harmony with God (cf. Eph. **1**.9 f.), He delivers His sovereignty to God who bestowed it on Him. But if His kingship comes to an end in its present phase, it is only to emerge in the eternal Kingdom of God: there is no failure of the promise that His Kingdom will have no end (Isa. **9**.7; Luke **1**.33). His present kingship is the appointed means for the consummation of that rule of God which He inaugurated by the completion of His work on earth. The humble submissiveness which characterized Him then continues to characterize Him at the consummation, when He is still seen subject to the One who gave Him universal dominion.

What is involved in the destruction of the last enemy is elaborated in vs. 35–50. As the body that dies shares the nature of the mortal Adam, the man of earth, so the body that comes alive in resurrection shares the image of the immortal Christ, the heavenly man, who is Himself the image of God (2 Cor. **4**.4; Col. **1**.15). It has been God's eternal purpose that His people should be 'conformed to the image of his Son' (Rom. **8**.29); here we see how that purpose attains fulfilment.

Meditation 'Because He is Son, His highest reward and joy will consist in being subjected to the Father's supremacy' (T. C. Edwards).

Questions and themes for study and discussion on Studies 19-28

1. Are you conscious of any tension between our Lord's teaching about God as King and His teaching about God as Father?

2. 'The expression, "the kingdom of God", although used in many cases as synonymous with the kingdom of heaven, is to be distinguished from it in some instances' (*Scofield Reference Bible*). Do you agree?

3. 'Do not lay up for yourselves treasures on earth' (Matt. **6**.19). Does this prohibition mean, as has sometimes been said, that investing money for the future is as much forbidden to Jesus' followers as murder or adultery? If our answer is 'No', can we justify that answer?

4. Leaven is frequently used in the Bible as a figure of corruption (e.g. 1 Cor. **5**.6–8). It is sometimes urged that the leaven in the parable of Matt. **13**.33 should be understood in this way. What would the parable mean if this were so? What is your opinion of this interpretation?

5. In facing some of Jesus' 'hard sayings' there is a tendency to argue that He was using poetic hyperbole in order to drive His lesson more effectively home. We take this for granted in the saying about the camel and the needle's eye in Luke **18**.25; what shall we say of those who would treat the parable of the unforgiving servant (Matt. **18**.23–35) in this way?

6. Are the Old Testament prophecies about the coming King sitting on the throne of David fulfilled in Christ now? If so, how are we to understand 'the throne of David'?

7. Neither in the prescribed readings nor in the notes in this series of studies is any mention made of the thousand years' reign of Rev. **20**.4. Do you regard its omission as a serious defect? If so, how would you fit it into the picture here presented? How would you relate it, for instance, to 1 Cor. **15**.20–28?

FIVE

The Nature of the New Testament Church

29: 'I will build my church'

Matthew 12.46–50; 16.13–20

The former of these two passages introduces a new and spiritual family, replacing that of the natural order. The kinsfolk of Jesus in this new order are those who do the will of the heavenly Father (cf. Mark 3.35; also Luke 11.28, 'those who hear the word of God and keep it'). The disciples who adhered to Him during His earthly ministry were both the faithful remnant of the old Israel and the nucleus of the people of God in the new age. We have seen how Isaiah's disciples formed a faithful remnant in an earlier day (Isa. 8.16–18); the Isaiah passage is treated as an anticipation of Jesus' spiritual family in Heb. 2.13.

In Matt. 16.18 the same community is introduced, this time by means of the term 'church'. A rabbinical commentary on Isa. 51.1 f. ('look to the rock . . ., look to Abraham . . .'), explaining why Abraham is there given the title 'rock', relates a parable about a king who wished to build a stable structure and dug deep for a foundation, but for a long time found nothing but morass. When at last his workmen struck rock, he said, 'Now I can make a beginning!' So, it is implied, did God with Abraham, and so, according to Matthew, did Jesus with Peter. Finding a man who by inward revelation and not by hearsay testimony confessed Him as the Messiah, He says in effect, 'Now I have a foundation on which I can begin to build my Church!' It is best, when trying to understand Jesus' words to Peter, to forget about Rome and the Papacy as completely as possible. The confession of Jesus' person is the basis of His Church: the first confessor, with his fellow-confessors among the disciples, constitutes the foundation-stone (cf. Eph. 2.20, 'the foundation of the apostles and prophets'). The authority conferred on Peter in v. 19 is shared with his companions in 18.18; it includes the authority to proclaim effectively the gospel of forgiveness (with its corollary of judgement) to those outside the Church and to exercise discipline on those inside (cf. John 20.23).

Question: From these passages what appears as the condition for membership of the Church? Is anything further necessary or desirable?

30: The One Flock

John 10.1–30

The parable of the shepherd and the sheep is closely related to the immediately preceding narrative of John's Gospel. At the end of ch. 8 Jesus has been rejected from the fellowship of Israel; at the end of ch. 9 the man whom He cured of his blindness is cast out for confessing Him, but on being cast out he is found by Jesus and acknowledges Him as the Son of Man (or Son of God). He thus becomes one of the sheep whom the good shepherd calls out of the Jewish fold.

The language of ch. 10 echoes that of Ezek. 34, where God speaks as the Shepherd of Israel, the owner and guardian of His sheep, searching them out, rescuing them and caring for them. Instead of the unworthy shepherds who have fleeced the sheep, He says, 'I will set up over them one shepherd, my servant David, and he shall feed them' (23). 'My servant David' is the Messiah of David's line; by calling Himself the good shepherd, Jesus is tacitly claiming to be the Messiah.

It is important to distinguish between the fold (1, 16a) and the flock (16b). The fold is an enclosure which contains a restricted number of sheep. The flock has no external boundaries; the sheep which belong to it are kept together by following the shepherd, who is their leader and protector. When Jesus calls His own sheep out of the Jewish fold, He goes on to call from the surrounding hills His other sheep, which never belonged to that fold. Henceforth, with His former Jewish and former Gentile sheep united, there will be 'one flock' under 'one shepherd' (16b). But before this can happen, the good shepherd must lay down His life for the sheep (11).

There is a remarkable parallel to this in non-figurative language when John later interprets the high priest's prophecy (11.50) to mean that 'Jesus should die for the nation, and not for the nation only, but to gather into one the children of God who are scattered abroad' (11.51 f.).

Meditation:

> *Yet millions still uncalled remain*
> *Wide wandering in the wilderness,*
> *Thee, Saviour, let Thy love constrain*
> *To bring in every sheep that strays:*
>
> . . .
>
> *For Thy own gracious promise' sake*
> *Thou wilt incline their hearts to obey,*
> *One undivided people make,*
> *And give us all one perfect way.*

(C. Wesley)

31: The Fellowship of Reconciliation

Ephesians 1.1–14; 3.20, 21

Reconciliation is a master-theme of Colossians and Ephesians. In Colossians it is by the death of Christ that the world is reconciled to God; in Ephesians it is by that same death that conflicting groups of the human family are reconciled to each other. In particular, the mutual reconciliation of Jews and Gentiles in the Church is so wonderful an object of contemplation for Paul that in Ephesians he views the Church as God's pilot scheme for the reconciled universe of the future, when He accomplishes His 'plan for the fullness of time', to unite all things in Christ (1.10).

In 1.11–14 'we who first hoped in Christ', believers of Jewish birth, are distinguished from 'you also', believers of Gentile birth; but all distinction between them disappears now that they are united in Christ. Both alike have been sealed with the Spirit, who is 'the Holy Spirit of promise' not only in the sense of being 'the promised Holy Spirit' (13, RSV) but also in the sense of His personally constituting the 'promise' or 'guarantee' that believers will attain the full heritage of glory that awaits them. He is the 'guarantee' in the sense of being a 'first instalment' or 'initial down-payment' of all the bliss that lies in store for the people of God. This aspect of the Spirit's ministry is Paul's distinctive contribution to the New Testament doctrine of the Spirit.

The Church's present reconciliation and sealing with the Spirit, together with her coming glory, were decreed by God's predestinating grace before the world's foundation—that grace which became effective with the coming of Christ to earth and the securing of 'redemption through his blood' (1.7). God's eternal purpose, hidden for long ages, has now been disclosed: 'mystery'

41

(1.9) in the New Testament regularly means something previously concealed which has at length been revealed (cf. 3.3–12). As he ponders this mystery of worldwide reconciliation Paul is moved first to a prayer that his readers may have power to grasp it (3.14–19) and then to a spontaneous outburst of praise to the One who has conceived so breath-taking a consummation (3.20 f.). In the 'heavenly places' God is eternally glorified, but here and now on earth He may be glorified in His people.

Question: 'He chose us in him before the foundation of the world' (1.4). *Is this an invitation to relax or a challenge to press on?*

32: 'Christ loved the church'

Ephesians 5.21–33

In first-century Christianity ethical instructions, whether delivered orally or in writing, appear to have been grouped under such captions as 'Put off' (cf. 4.22), 'Put on' (cf. 4.24), 'Be subject' (cf. 5.21) and 'Watch and pray' (cf. 6.18 ff.). Several New Testament letters exhibit some at least of these captions. Our present reading forms the opening paragraph of the section headed 'Be subject'. Mutual deference among members of the Church is enjoined, and then it is given special application in the Christian household (cf. Col. 3.18 ff.). The simple statement of the mutual responsibilities of wives and husbands which we find elsewhere in the New Testament is here amplified by the presentation of this unique relationship as a picture of the relationship between Christ and the Church. The phrase 'as to the Lord' does not mean that wives should yield to their husbands that obedience which, as Christians, they owe to Christ, but rather that deference to their husbands is a duty they owe to the Lord, as the husbands' love for their wives is a duty which they for their part owe to Him.

If, as Paul has said in 1 Cor. 11.3, 'the head of a woman is her husband' and, as he has said in Eph. 1.22 f., Christ is head of the Church, an analogy can be drawn between the two headships. As Christ loves the Church and protects her, so let the husband love and protect his wife. As the Church is submissive to Christ, so let a wife be submissive to her husband. As Christ and the Church form a living unity, so husband and wife constitute 'one flesh', as is said in the primeval ordinance of Gen. 2.24.

The description of Christ's love for the Church (25 ff.) goes beyond a husband's normal love for his wife. Not only has He sacrificed His life for the Church but it is His purpose so to cleanse and sanctify her that she may be His spotless and glorious bride (cf. 2 Cor. 11.2). The 'washing' of v. 26 is baptism which is the seal of the inner cleansing of the Holy Spirit and the 'word' probably the invocation or confession of Christ as Lord (cf. Acts 22.16), here transferred from the individual believer to the believing community. The portrayal of the Church in v. 27 corresponds not to present reality but to future destiny: the Church militant here on earth bears many a scar and stain from her warfare but the Church triumphant is purified from 'any such thing'.

Meditation:

> *By faith we see the glory*
> *To which Thou shalt restore us,*
> *The cross despise for that high prize*
> *Which Thou hast set before us.*
> *And if Thou count us worthy,*
> *We each, as dying Stephen,*
> *Shall see Thee stand at God's right hand*
> *To take us up to heaven.*

(C. Wesley).

33: City of the Living God

Hebrews 12.18–29

As Israel in Moses' day stood to meet God at the foot of Sinai (Exod. 19.17), so the people of God now come to the heavenly Zion, for a confrontation which is more gracious to those who are sprinkled by the covenant blood but more terrible to those who refuse to hear Him who 'warns from heaven' (25).

This is the well-founded city to which Abraham looked forward (11.10), the new Jerusalem to which men of faith have access now. The 'innumerable angels in festal gathering' (22) are attendants on God and, by His commission, ministrants to His people (1.14); when believers come to them it is not to worship them but to worship the God whom they serve. The 'assembly of the first-born' (23) is probably the whole communion of saints, whether triumphant in heaven or militant on earth. To this assembly believers have come—not merely into its presence but into its membership. All the people of Christ are 'first-born' through their union with Him who is *the* First-born; let them not barter their birthright away, as Esau did (16 f.). Even those who are bound to God by the new covenant must not forget that He is judge. He is the vindicator and defender of His people, but even His people—especially His people—will incur His judgement if they despise His saving message (cf. **10**.30). The 'spirits of just men made perfect' are the believers of pre-Christian days who could not be 'made perfect' apart from us (**11**.40) but have now entered into the rest of God towards which they pressed. Above all, believers have come to Jesus, whose sacrifice cleanses the conscience and, unlike the vengeance-demanding blood of Abel (Gen. **4**.10), brings assurance of pardon and peace (24).

As God brought the material universe into being by His word (cf. **1**.3; **11**.3), so in due course He will shake it out of existence (Hag. **2**.6); but He has given His Church an unshakable Kingdom which will endure when all things sublunary disappear and 'leave not a wrack behind'. For this let us be grateful, and let our gratitude take the form of acceptable worship to God. 'The city of God remaineth.'

Meditation:
> *Who can behold the blazing light ?*
> *Who can approach consuming flame ?*
> *None but Thy wisdom knows Thy might;*
> *None but Thy word can speak Thy name.*

(I. Watts)

34: Spiritual Temple and Holy Priesthood
1 Peter 1.22–2.10

There is a widely held belief that this epistle, or at least the first part of it, has especially in view new converts to Christianity, perhaps on the occasion of their baptism. Peter wishes them to know and practise the way of life which befits the people of Christ, and also to appreciate the nobility of the heritage which they are entering. Pagan vices must be put away; Christian graces must be cultivated. Whereas other New Testament writers rebuke their readers for being fit for nothing but milk when they should be able to assimilate solid food (1 Cor. **3**.1 ff.; Heb. **5**.12 ff.),

Peter, using the metaphor a little differently, encourages his readers to acquire an appetite for 'pure spiritual milk' and so become healthy in soul (2.2).

The new community of which they have become members is described in various figures drawn from the Old Testament, but chiefly as a temple built upon the 'living stone' who is Christ Himself (cf. Eph. 2.20). Isa. 28.16 and Psa. 118.22 are quoted as 'testimonies' to Him in this regard. The 'preciousness' of the stone in Isa. 28.16 is experienced by believers; unbelievers, on the contrary, find in Him a stumbling stone, as their predecessors did in Isaiah's day (Isa. 8.14). In the new temple believers are 'living stones' or, by a change of metaphor, 'a holy priesthood' (2.5). The sacrifices offered by the priesthood in this temple are appropriately 'spiritual sacrifices'—the sacrifices of thanksgiving and generosity (Heb. 13.15 f.) and the celebration of God's saving deeds (2.9). As in Rom. 9.25 f. (see Study 18), the lesson of the story of Hosea now finds expression anew on a world-wide scale: Gentiles who were formerly excluded from the community of God's people and from all share in His covenant mercy are now acknowledged as 'God's own people' and hailed as His 'royal priesthood' and 'holy nation' in terms once addressed to Israel encamped before God at Sinai (Exod. 19.6). So we come back to the starting-point of our present series of studies—but how much has happened in between!

For further thought: The call to mutual love within the Christian brotherhood (1.22) is found in practically every New Testament writer. Does it have the same prominence, in theory or in practice, in the Church today? How damaging is this lack, if it exists, to the life and activities of the Christian community?

Questions and themes for study and discussion on Studies 29-34

1. Consider the implications of the theme of a church conference several years ago: 'The Servant Lord and His Servant People.'
2. In what ways is the Church of New Testament days continuous with Israel and in what ways does it mark a new beginning?
3. 'The Church is God's instrument for bringing in the Kingdom.' Assess the adequacy and biblical basis of this statement.

4. Collect the images under which the Church is set forth in the New Testament. Consider how they contribute to our fuller appreciation of the 'manifold wisdom of God' made known through the Church (Eph. 3.10).
5. With the aid of a concordance, collect the New Testament passages which speak of Christ as the 'corner stone' or something similar. How do they help us to understand the relation between Christ and the Church?

SIX

One Body in Christ

35: 'I in them and thou in me'

John 17

Since David Chytraeus in the 16th century first called this our Lord's 'high-priestly prayer', many have followed his example. A considerable part of John 17 consists of intercession for those whom our Lord was about to leave behind in the 'world'. This was the scripture from which pre-eminently John Knox learned his doctrine of the Church and where, as he said on his deathbed, 'I cast my first anchor'.

Here Jesus turns aside from conversing with His disciples to hold communion with His Father. The hour of His sacrifice, which in this Gospel is also the hour of His glory, has come at last, and so completely dedicated is He to the fulfilment by this means of His Father's will that He can speak of having 'accomplished' the work given Him to do (4). His perspective is beyond death: 'I am no more in the world,' He says (11).

The language which He uses here about His followers is different from that of John 10, where He speaks of them as the sheep whose Shepherd He is; but the sense is basically the same. They have been called out from the 'world' (i.e. the unbelieving mass) to form a new community; yet the 'world', to which they no longer belong (16), remains the environment in which they are to live and witness (11, 18). Nor will their witness be ineffective; others will believe in Him 'through their word' (20), and these also are included in His intercession. The purpose of His intercession is their unity—a unity reflecting that between the Father and the Son (21, cf. 10.30). This can be achieved only as He is present in them, not only as individuals but as a community. If He, who is one with the Father, lives in them by His Spirit, and so binds them together, we have the co-inherence of v. 23; 'I in them and thou in me, that they may become perfectly one'. It is a spiritual unity indeed, but a visible unity also: it must be seen by the world, so that the world may have credible evidence of the validity of Jesus' claim to be the sent one of God, the object of His Father's love, as His people also are.

47

The world is not written off as beyond redemption; it is to be brought to faith through the living testimony of the followers of Jesus. The glory concerning which He prays in v. 24 is the fullness of that divine and reciprocal love which they have already begun to enjoy and exhibit; it is nothing less than the Beatific Vision.

Meditation: 'We are called to be "partakers of the divine nature" (*2 Pet. 1.4*), *of that love which is the essence of Deity'* (W. Temple).

36: 'All things in common'

Acts 2.41–47; 4.32–5.11

What Jesus prayed for on the night of His betrayal (John **17**) began to be realized with the descent of the Spirit. There is a vital continuity between the Old Testament people of God and those of the New Testament; but in the meantime the Church has died and been raised again with her Lord, and it is as a new creation, indwelt by the Spirit, that she enters the new age. Those who believed in Jesus through His disciples' witness (John **17**.20) suddenly became several thousand strong, and as He prayed that they might be one (John **17**.21), now we are told that 'all who believed were together' (**2**.44). Their 'togetherness' was manifested in their baptism, in their adherence to the apostles' teaching and fellowship, in the breaking of bread and the prayers, and in their spontaneous community of goods (**2**.44 f.; **4**.32). Prudent commentators argue that this last state of affairs could not go on indefinitely, and that even at the time it had certain disadvantages; but Luke's narrative has nothing but commendation for those who expressed their new and exhilarating sense of oneness in this way. Other pious communities in Israel had all things in common; why should the followers of Jesus fall behind them? He Himself had set little store by private property, and indeed during His ministry He and His closest disciples appear to have practised community of such goods as they had. What is important, however, is the vital reality of their fellowship rather than the particular manner in which it was expressed. Was there not a danger that some members of the group might imitate the external generosity without experiencing the inward unity of heart? There was indeed; such a danger can never be separated from the externals of religion. Not only generosity, but martyrdom itself, acquires Christian value only as it is the manifestation of genuine love within (1 Cor. **13**.3).

Thus in **4.32–5.11** we have the opposing examples of Barnabas and Ananias. Perhaps Barnabas' gift excited such admiration in the community that Ananias and Sapphira decided to emulate his action. Had Barnabas' gift been made for the sake of admiration or commendation it would have been no more creditable than theirs; but their dubious motivation betrayed itself in their pretence to be a little more generous than they actually were. It is a mercy that the same judgement is not meted out today on those who give for the sake of appearance and not out of pure love.

Question: To what extent can the picture of the primitive Church in Acts 2.41–47 be taken as a pattern for the Church today?

37: Diversity in Unity

1 Corinthians 12

Paul takes up a problem current in one local church, and deals with it in such a way as to bring out principles of abiding relevance to all churches. There was a tendency in the church of Corinth to emphasize the importance of one particular category of spiritual gift—that which was specially spectacular and impressive. Paul corrects this tendency by stressing that the importance of spiritual gifts in the church is to be assessed by their contribution to the life and health of the believing community. A wide variety of gifts or ministries is necessary if all the community's needs are to be supplied. The capacity to exercise these various ministries is bestowed by the Holy Spirit on various members of the church, and they are to be cultivated for the well-being of the whole. Paul brings this out by comparing the local church to a body—the body of Christ (27)—in which the individual believers are the limbs and organs, performing their appropriate functions. The health of the body depends on the harmonious functioning of all the parts, whether external or internal, whether highly regarded or of little account. The malfunctioning of the most inconspicuous part will impair the health of the whole body, and a breakdown of co-ordination between the parts will produce distressing symptoms.

This is the only place in the Pauline letters where baptism in the Spirit is mentioned (13); it denotes the divine act by which believers, instead of being left as isolated individuals, are incorporated as fellow-members in the body of Christ.

Perhaps the analogy of the body commended itself to Paul the more readily because of his Damascus-road experience, when the exalted Lord challenged him with the question: 'why do you persecute me?' (Acts 9.4). When any part of the body is hurt, it is the head that complains, and this is what happened when Paul was engaged in persecuting the 'members of Christ' (as he calls Christians in 1 Cor. 6.15). In the church, then, for all the members to opt for the more public or specialized ministries will mean a one-sided development. Unity and growth will be promoted better by the cultivation of a wide variety of 'gifts', where the person who gives out hymnbooks has parity of esteem with the preacher in the pulpit or the leader of the choir.

Question: The confession 'Jesus is Lord' (3) has been described as the Church's original and still sufficient creed. Would you agree with this?

38: A Matter of Equality

2 Corinthians 8

The interdependence of the various parts of the body may illustrate not only relations within one church but relations between churches. Paul was specially concerned that the Gentile churches which he founded should maintain a sense of fellowship with the mother church of Jerusalem, with which they had little direct contact. Paul himself had never been a resident member of the Jerusalem church, and indeed his relations with it were sometimes strained; but it was the mother church of Christendom and as such was entitled to special recognition. From Jerusalem the gospel had gone forth in the first instance, even if now it was mainly involved in Jewish evangelization. Paul knew that if fellowship was not preserved between his Gentile mission and the Jerusalem church, a disastrous cleavage might ensue within the Christian ranks.

The Gentile churches were not in a position to confer on Jerusalem the sort of spiritual benefit they had received from it, but the Jerusalem believers suffered from chronic poverty, and they could do something to relieve this. At an earlier date the first Gentile church (that of Antioch) had shown its sense of responsibility in this regard by sending a gift to Jerusalem during a famine (Acts 11.29 f.). It was perhaps then that the Jerusalem leaders begged Paul and Barnabas to continue to 'remember the poor'—'which very thing,' says Paul, 'I was eager to do' (Gal. 2.10). So now, some ten years later, he organized a collection throughout his Gentile mission-field to relieve the poverty of the Jerusalem Christians and bind them more closely to their Gentile brothers. He had mentioned it to the Corinthian Christians earlier (1 Cor. 16.1–4), but difficult personal relations had intervened, so now he raises it afresh. To stimulate their generosity he refers to the liberal contributions made by the impoverished Macedonian churches; above all, he refers to the Lord's supreme example of self-giving when He became poor so that His people might be enriched (9). Titus had recently accomplished a delicate commission for Paul in Corinth (7.6–15); now Paul sends him back there, with two companions, to help the Corinthians to complete their contribution to the Jerusalem fund.

Thought: Consider Paul's re-wording in v. 12 of the principle enshrined in the incident of the widow's 'mite' (Mark 12.41–44). Is not this giving according to the law of the Kingdom?

39: Liberal Sowing, Liberal Reaping

2 Corinthians 9

Paul devotes all his resources of diplomacy and persuasiveness to ensure a generous response from the Corinthians. It was of the essence of the gift that it should be voluntary and spontaneous; hence he could not press them to give (7). He knew, moreover, that his opponents would misrepresent his motives in raising this large sum of money; hence he scrupulously avoided handling any of it himself, and arranged that it should be taken to Jerusalem by delegates of the contributing churches, whom he planned to accompany. As in ch. 8 he stimulated the Corinthians by the example of the Macedonians' generosity, so now he reveals that he has used the Corinthians' example to encourage the Macedonians. 'I have boasted to them about you, telling them that Achaia (the province of which Corinth was the seat of administration) was ready last year; it would never do, then, for representatives of the Macedonian churches to come with me to Corinth and find you not ready even now. *I* should feel embarrassed after all my confident boasting about you, to say nothing of *your* embarrassment!' (4).

The principle that those who give more receive more, attested in the Old Testament, is invoked in vs. 6 ff.; if the Corinthians give generously on this occasion, their reward will be such enrichment that they will be able to give with still greater generosity in future.

In secular life it often happens that the receiving of favours arouses in the recipient feelings of resentment towards the donor (as more affluent nations today have learned, foreign aid programmes do not ensure the good will or gratitude of those who benefit by them). Paul cannot conceive of such a reaction in the Christian community. The Jerusalem Christians will be so appreciative of the Gentiles' generosity that they will be driven to increased prayer on their behalf, thankful for this new bond of affection. Generosity on the one hand and gratitude on the other are manifestations of God's 'surpassing grace' in His people, their response to His 'unspeakable gift'.

The subject of these two chapters is not remote from 'Kingdom truth' and 'Church doctrine'; generous giving characterizes the King of the Kingdom and the Lord of the Church.

Thought: 'In the New Testament, religion is grace, and ethics is gratitude' (Thomas Erskine).

40: 'Baptized into Christ'

Galatians 3.23–29; Colossians 3.9–17

To be 'baptized into Christ' (Gal. 3.27) is identical with being 'baptized into one body' (1 Cor. 12.13). Differences of race, social status or sex, however important they may be in other spheres, are transcended 'in Christ', i.e. in the Christian fellowship (Gal. 3.28). Attempts are sometimes made to press a distinction between what is true 'in Christ' and what obtains 'in the church'; but it is precisely in the church that the features of the new order in Christ are to be put into practical effect. As for the three distinctions which Paul finds transcended in Christ, they correspond to three things for which Jewish men have thanked God day by day for hundreds of years—not to have been born a Gentile, a slave or a woman. Paul, who may himself have formerly used such words in thanksgiving, now finds the distinctions to which they refer irrelevant in Christ.

Similarly in Col. 3.11 he affirms that such distinctions disappear in the new humanity; if Christ is everything, living in all His people, then national, cultural and religious cleavages are bridged.

To 'put on' Christ (Gal. **3**.27) means to display the graces which characterize Him and which are therefore fitting for His people to wear (cf. Rom. **13**.14). What this means is spelt out in greater detail in Col. **3**.12 ff. Putting off the old humanity (9)—the old Adam nature—means the renouncing of pagan vices, such as those listed in vs. 5–8; putting on the new humanity means the cultivation of the Christian graces listed in vs. 12–16 and making v. 17 the comprehensive rule of life. Since the Christian household provides the most congenial soil for their cultivation, the general injunctions of vs. 12–17 are followed by their particular application to family relationships (3.18–4.1). These relationships are not given a spiritual reference here as in Eph. **5**.21–33 (at which we have looked already); the maintenance of Christian family standards both pleases the Lord and presents a powerful witness in the world.

Question: Since the church is a Christian family 'writ large', can the injunctions of Col. 3.18–4.1 be reworded so as to apply to the mutual duties and responsibilities of church members?

41: 'Partnership in the gospel'

Philippians 1.1–11; 4.1–3

Paul's sense of unity with his converts was deep and far-reaching. When they prospered, he rejoiced; when dissension or similar trouble broke out among them, he was greatly distressed; when injury of any kind was done to them, his indignation was as keen as if it had been done to himself—indeed, it was keener, for he would have preferred to endure the injury himself, if they could thus be spared it. The Lord's assessment of Paul's apostolic service on the final day of review and reward would depend, he believed, on the quality of his converts' faith and life. Similarly, he encouraged them to regard themselves as partners with him in his Gentile mission, by prayer, by material support (cf. 4.10–18) and by other means. The response of the Philippian Christians to this encouragement filled him with joy. To a degree beyond many of his converts they felt that they had a share in furthering the enterprise to which he was committed. It was so when they were first converted; it was still so several years later when he sent them this letter; and he is assured that it will remain so until 'the day of Jesus Christ' (1.6). This assurance brings him great comfort in his present imprisonment; it is all part of what is involved in being 'in Christ'.

The practical implications of being 'in Christ', however, are displayed not only in relation to the furtherance of the gospel over a wide area, but also at grass-roots level, in inter-personal relations in a local Christian fellowship. Paul's concern for unity of love and purpose in the Philippian church finds expression in 2.2–8, where he points out that the best way to achieve like-mindedness is to cultivate the mind of Christ, the attitude of self-forgetfulness and self-emptying which was seen in Him personally and which may be seen in them as they are 'in Him' corporately. In 4.1–3 he carries on this thought, and ventures to name two Christian women who need to be reminded of it, confident that in the affection which binds him to his Philippian friends he will not give offence by doing so, and begs them to agree 'in the Lord'—as fellow-members of His body (4.2). With his entreaty goes an encomium, as he recalls how these two were foremost in practical co-operation with his gospel ministry. (The 'true yokefellow' of 4.3 may be Luke.) The large-scale and small-scale manifestations of Christian fellowship are mentioned together; both are of the essence of being 'one body in Christ'.

Meditation: 'I hold you in my heart' (1.7) is no doubt what Paul meant, but the words might equally well be rendered 'you hold me in your heart'—which we can well believe was also true. Is not this reciprocity of affection implicit in being 'one body in Christ'?

42: Life, Light and Love
1 John 1.1–5; 4.7–21

John's first letter was sent to a group of Christians in Asia Minor who were bewildered by the secession of some of their former associates, who regarded themselves as a spiritual *élite*. The seceders had embraced a new interpretation of Christianity in which it was difficult to recognize the gospel as they had originally received it; yet the seceders were so confident that they possessed the truth, that theirs was the way of eternal life, that the others were uneasy and wondered if they were right after all.

The Church is sent into the world to establish a beach-head for the Kingdom of God (cf. John 17.18), but in her conflict with a hostile environment she is assured of the presence and enabling power of the Son of Man, who endured and overcame.

Question: Who is he 'who can destroy both soul and body in hell' (28)?

45: Enduring Persecution, Bearing Witness
John 15.18–16.4

These words of Jesus are the Johannine counterpart to those at which we have looked in Matt. 10.16–42; John 15.20 refers back to the saying of Matt. 10.24. Here the words are appended to the parable of the true vine. John does not use Pauline language about the body and its members, but the same truth of the common life which the people of Christ derive from abiding union with Him is taught in terms of the vine and the branches. Now, however, come the practical implications of this union with Christ. 'The world' is 'the godless world' (as NEB renders it in 1 John 2.15), society organized not only without reference to God but in positive hostility to Him. The disciples have been chosen out of it and sent back into it (cf. 17.18). John's readers would think of their situation in regard to the persecuting Roman Empire, but in the first instance it is not the Gentile state that is meant here but the Jewish theocratic establishment, as is plain from 15.22–25 and the mention of expulsion from synagogues in 16.2a (cf. 9.22, 34). The statement in 16.2b, 'whoever kills you will think he is offering service to God', might almost have been spoken in advance about Saul of Tarsus (cf. Acts 22.3–5; 26.9–11). The disciples in fact had their first experience of opposition from the theocratic establishment which had denounced their Master to the Romans (cf. Acts 4.1 ff.; 5.17 ff.). In the eyes of Roman authorities, too, men who acknowledged themselves to be followers of One who was condemned for sedition in a Roman court could expect to be viewed with suspicion.

The Church, however, is in the world not only to endure persecution but to bear witness. It is not left to bear its witness unaided. As in Matt. 10.20 the Spirit of the Father speaks through those who are questioned regarding their faith, so here

59

'the Spirit of truth', proceeding from the Father, bears witness to Christ with and in their witness. There is a remarkable correspondence between the language of **15.26 f.** and that of Acts **5.32**, where the apostles, making their defence before the high priest and the Sanhedrin, tell how the rejected and crucified Jesus has been raised and exalted by God, and add: 'we are witnesses to these things, and so is the Holy Spirit whom God has given to those who obey him.'

*Thought: Consider the implication of **15.22**. The more privilege, the more responsibility.*

46: Obedience, Love, Wakefulness

Romans 13

Jesus' injunction to 'render to Caesar the things that are Caesar's' (Mark **12.17**) was an answer to a burning question, relating to a delicate situation in Judea which had no parallel outside that province. Paul's teaching in Rom. **13.1–7** about the Christian's attitude to the authorities may be regarded as a generalization and expansion of Jesus' injunction, but Paul's treatment of the subject exposed him to no jeopardy. He had, for the most part, happy experience of the benevolent neutrality of the imperial magistrates with whom he had had to deal up to the time of writing this letter: it was this experience, no doubt, that encouraged him two years later to appeal from the subordinate jurisdiction of the procurator of Judea to the supreme tribunal in Rome. There may have been some Christians who argued that, since they now belonged to the Kingdom of Christ, they owed allegiance to no earthly ruler. Paul corrects such an attitude by insisting that earthly rulers, while discharging their proper business, are God's servants and should therefore receive special respect from God's children. Accordingly, he says, 'pay all of them their dues' (7).

There is one thing which is due to all men from the Christian in the world: 'let the only debt you owe be the debt of love' (8). Jesus had already summarized the law of human relationships in terms of the commandment to love one's neighbour as oneself (Lev. **19.18**; cf. Mark **12.31**); Paul echoes Him: 'love is the fulfilling of the law' (10; cf. Gal. **5.14**).

The days were critical. Paul's reading of the signs of the times

60

was accurate. The persecution of the Church by Nero lay only seven years ahead; the Jewish revolt against Rome, nine years. The Church in the world must be alert. If crisis was near, so was deliverance; the time for witness was short and must be exploited to the full. The 'armour of light' (12) is both defensive (against temptation) and offensive (for the invasion of the realm of darkness). To 'put on the Lord Jesus Christ' (14) and so to reflect His character (cf. Gal. 3.27, Study 40) is the privilege of the Church in the world.

Question: Since 'love is the fulfilling of the law' (10), is it sufficient, with regard to any contemplated action, to ask whether or not it is done in love?

47: Consistent Christianity

2 Corinthians 6.14–7.1

In the atmosphere of Corinth there were two dominant features, interwoven the one with the other, which were totally inimical to Christian life and testimony: idolatry and fornication. It was not at all easy for members of the church in that city to keep themselves untainted by the one or the other. Paul had written more than one letter warning his converts against their blighting influence (cf. 1 Cor. 5.9–11; 6.9–18; 10.14–22), but he knew that his warnings had not been taken to heart by all. They for their part were aware that Paul knew this, and they had an uneasy feeling about it. In 2 Cor. 6.11–13 he has invited them to cast aside all reserve and open their hearts to him, as he opened his to them. He knew that there was this sense of reserve, and he knew its source: it was their consciousness that some of them were still attached to these pagan ways. So he digresses in this paragraph to bid them have done with such things once and for all. Why join with unbelievers in pursuits which were part of the pagan way of life but totally out of keeping with their Christian profession?

It is a curiosity of biblical interpretation that these verses, and especially v. 17, should so often have been misused as a pretext for the withdrawal of Christians from the society of their fellow-Christians. Disquieting as many tendencies in the church of Corinth were, Paul did not dream of telling the 'concerned' members of the church to secede and form a purer fellowship.

Rather, he urges them all to separate from idolatry and all associations which might lead them into it. The call is not to the faithful to cleanse themselves from the others, but to the whole church to cleanse itself from every defiling influence and so have their sanctification brought to completion. Thus they will be known as the sons and daughters of God, who is Himself the all-holy One.

Question: Is secession from the church ever justified?

48: Living by the Will of God

1 Peter 2.11–17; 3.8–4.6

Peter has told the new Christians to whom he writes something of the glory of the heritage which they have entered. Now he tells them of the kind of life they are to live as 'exiles of the Dispersion' (1.1). Just as Jews of the Dispersion maintained their ancestral way of life among the Gentiles, so the Church must maintain the Christian way of life in an environment where this is something novel. He himself writes to them from 'Babylon', the archetypal place of exile for the people of God (5.13).

Above all, they must live in such a way as not to bring the Christian name into disrepute. They cannot avoid criticism for being Christians, and scandalous rumours will circulate about their anti-social conduct; but their behaviour must give no colour to such rumours, but rather confute their critics and lead them to a truer assessment. Both within the brotherhood (3.8) and outside it (3.9) their attitude to others must conform to their profession; the Sermon on the Mount is echoed in 3.9. Psa. 34, from which comes the quotation in 3.10–12, was early used at Christian baptismal services (cf. 2.3, which echoes Psa. 34.8).

The injunction at the end of 3.14 and beginning of 3.15 is adapted from Isa. 8.12 f., but whereas it is the Lord of hosts who is to be 'sanctified' there, here it is Christ as Lord. This is not the only place in the New Testament where Old Testament passages referring to the God of Israel are applied to Jesus—an incidental testimony to His first followers' spontaneous recognition of His divine nature.

If Christians are called upon to suffer for righteousness' sake, they have their Lord's example to encourage them. Their baptism means that they are united to Him as the risen and exalted One (3.21 f.); as they confess Him in word then, so let them confess Him in deed at all times. The world might ask: 'What good does your confession do you, if you suffer martyrdom?' So it might be asked of all believers who have died since conversion what good it did them, since they died like other men. Peter replies that, while they did indeed die like other men, yet because of their conversion they have attained spiritual life— a share in the life of God (4.6). So all who enter into the Christian fellowship must bid farewell to their unregenerate past and live henceforth as witnesses to Christ in the world: this is to live 'by the will of God' (4.2).

Question: In what forms can we defend our Christian hope in the western world today?

Questions and themes for study and discussion on Studies 44-48

1. Is persecution by the world a constant 'note' of the true Church? Or should the Church expect by its continuous and consistent witness to win the world ultimately for Christ, so that persecution may become a thing of the past? What bearing has the hope of a reconciled universe (e.g. in Col. 1.19 f.) on this question?

2. The 'governing authorities' of Rom. 13.1 were for Paul and his first readers those who held office under the Roman Empire. How do you reconcile with his statement that they 'have been instituted by God' the picture in Rev. 13.2, where the same Empire, in a later phase of its development, seems to receive its authority from the great red dragon? Are there some governments on earth today which Christians should regard in terms of Rev. 13 rather than in terms of Rom. 13?

3. In the light of such a passage as 1 Pet. 2.13–17, is it ever right for Christians to take part in liberation or resistance movements—movements, for example, aimed at the overthrow or expulsion of an oppressive enemy power? Does our Lord's aloofness from the Zealot movement provide guidance here? What about passive resistance?

4. 'The world' for me is the environment in which I live and work. What is my responsibility in it as an heir of the Kingdom of God and a member of the Church of Christ?